The practices, suggestions, and techniques
presented in this book are not intended to be
substituted for or construed as medical diagnosis,
advice, or treatment. Always consult with a qualified
physician before starting this or any new wellness
program. The author assumes no responsibility
for injuries acquired during the implementation
of these practices, suggestions, and techniques.

To paraphrase the *Ayurvedic* physician
and sage Charaka, we are called upon to enter into the
heart of others with the virtue of light and love in order
to truly know and serve them, and ourselves.

John, Sam, Mom, Dad, Marina, and Lorraine,
this book is dedicated to you with gratitude and Great
Love for showing me what this means, every day.

Namaste.

The Yogic Path

To paraphrase the *Ayurvedic* physician and sage Charaka, we are called upon to enter into the heart of others with the virtue of light and love in order to truly know and serve them, and ourselves. The moment I stepped onto a yoga mat, I knew this to be true, and over the past nearly-fifteen years this philosophy has become a living invocation for me through my work in the world as a Hatha Yoga practitioner, instructor, and studio owner. My purpose for writing *Sutras Through the Seasons* has been no different: it is an offering, an invitation into all that I have come to know as the wholeness of living deeply through the second-century text, *The Yoga Sutras of Patanjali.*

Intended for the practitioner and non-practitioner alike, *Sutras Through the Seasons* seeks to divine from and reframe classical yogic teachings for the everyday.

Unlike any other rereading of the *Yoga Sutras*, I have grouped selections from Patanjali's text (the translations of which are informed by those of T. K. V. Desikachar and Swami Jnaneshvara Bharati) into six emerging themes that speak to the conditions and conditioning of a culture that continues to compromise our wellness and wellbeing in the West. These themes – awareness, intention, purpose, surrender, healing, and consciousness – represent the layers of self in a progressive, inward-moving framework of chapters that lead one towards personal transformation.

Designed as a focus for a week or a month at a time, each chapter's translation of the *Sutras* is followed by a meditation on one of these "layers of self", a series of reflective questions and affirmations, as well as supporting, complementary *asana* (body work), *pranayama* (breath work), and *dhyana* (mind work) techniques that align with the "seasonal" evolution of the bodymind according to *Ayurveda* (the "science of life"). I see the Yogic Path, therefore, as a journey through three "seasons" of unfolding: *kapha* – our spring or childhood – as being our time of growth, development, exploration, and learning; *pitta* – our summer or early adulthood – as being our time of ambition, affirmation, and establishment; and *vata* – our autumn into winter, or late adulthood – as being our time of expansion and liberation. The Yogic Path does not demand perfection along this journey, it asks for practice; as with the seasons, we often find ourselves beginning again and again in life – but it is always the beginning again, the practice, that counts in the end. *Sutras Through the Seasons* is a companion to this pursuit – a book to pick up and finish, again and again, as we take on a more full expression of the self with each reading, each beginning.

The market today is beginning to point to this cultural desire to begin again, and is currently driven by methods for developing mindfulness backed by neurological research. World-renowned neuroscientist Richie Davidson, founder of the Center for Investigating Healthy Minds at the University of Wisconsin-Madison, is a passionate advocate for mindfulness and the evidence in neuroscience that supports it; as his findings demonstrate, such practices give us the power to establish and strengthen desired neural pathways in the brain that directly impact behaviour, emotion, processing, perception – even gene-expression. What Davidson's research concludes, then, is that wellbeing is, in fact, a skill that can be learned[1]. As it turns out, wellness, like mindfulness, is not something that we acquire but rather something that we practice – sometimes through the beginning again and again. This conviction, unlike that found in quick-fix approaches, is at the heart of *Sutras Through the Seasons*.

I feel passionately that health, happiness, and healing are not part of a wheel to be reinvented, but one to be rediscovered through the wisdom of the ancient texts

that have long been available to us, just waiting to be reimagined for today. Such is the case with Patanjali's teachings in the *Yoga Sutras*, in which we find not the currently commercialized "what to do" of mindfulness but the thousands-year old "how to be" of it. Mindfulness, therefore, is central to *Sutras Through the Seasons* and to what I mean when I say the "wholeness of living deeply"; it is not just the "doing" of a five minute breathing exercise or a guided meditation app, it is the moment-to-moment "being" of a way of life.

With forty-two percent of U.S. adults admitting in a recent American Psychological Association study to feeling like they are not able to effectively manage their stress levels, as well as to symptoms of irritability, anxiety, exhaustion, and depression[2], it is clear that there is a population of people struggling to find an entry-point into such a life. It is in this way that *Sutras Through the Seasons* has the potential to extend beyond the yoga *sangha* (which includes more than twenty million practitioners in the United States alone[3]) to embrace a community of seekers in need of real change.

It is my belief that *Sutras Through the Seasons* is the grounding for this change, for a life of present moments – and, as the musician Miten reminds us, "Being present is the ultimate expression of love." To live mindfully, then, is our highest calling.

It is clear that the West is ready to redefine what it has come to think of as fulfillment. My response to, and, more importantly, my living experience of, this shift is *Sutras Through the Seasons* – my offering. Because it was created in the spirit of making the Yogic Path an accessible, inclusive, comprehensive, and sustainable practice of evolution for all who come to it, my vision for *Sutras Through the Seasons* is that its form will be a reflection of this; it is not another volume to rest on the bookshelf, but a companion to rest in one's hands. It is my hope that *Sutras Through the Seasons* lies always at the ready, whether it be on the nightstand, in the backpack, or by the meditation stool. Accompanied with photography from my travels through the temples of Thailand, it is my intention that my work also be as much a visual journey as a reading one.

My ten years as a Special Education teacher in the public, Montessori, and independent school systems, my co-instruction of a yoga and sutra study program and committee work for the implementation of a comprehensive mind, body, and spiritual wellness program at a co-ed university prep institution, my service at local shelters, my instruction of private and group classes out of my home studio, The Village Yoga Studio – all of this experience has led me to the understanding that the need for wholeness, for living deeply, does not discriminate across demographics; it is alive in and essential to us all. Having studied the production, circulation, and cultural relevance of texts during my M.A., I also know the power of the word and the remarkable ways in which it can imprint upon us a living text – one that changes as we do the more we come back to it and read it. *Sutras Through the Seasons* is an invitation to know such a text; as we surrender to the support of the meditations and practices inspired by the teachings of Patanjali, we find that we are carrying them with us as much as they are carrying us.

And so it begins.

Namaste,

Erin Holtz Braeckman

May 2016

[1] "Stalking the Meditating Brain", *Mindful* magazine, August 2014.
[2] "Stress in America" 2014, American Psychological Association, www.apa.org.
[3] "Yoga in America" 2012, Sports Marketing Surveys USA and *Yoga Journal* magazine, www.yogajournal.com.

Kapha Season

In the *Ayurvedic* cycle of life, *kapha* is the
"season" of childhood, a foundational time of
growth, development, exploration, and
learning. Similarly, we now enter the *Kapha
Season* of our Yogic Path, challenging such
kapha imbalances as attachment and
identification while affirming the qualities of
stability and loving-kindness through the
practices of awareness and intention.

~ Moving Inwards:
Meditations on Awareness ~
Sutras 1.1-1.17:

1.1   Now begin the teachings on the path to Yoga.

1.2   Yoga [or Union] is the redirection of the mind without distraction.

1.3   In this state, one acts from a place of clear and right perception – from one's true nature.

1.4   Otherwise, one invests in and identifies with one's thoughts; with the projections and preconceptions of the ego.

1.8   Misapprehension [one of the five activities of the mind, including comprehension, imagination, deep sleep, and memory] is false observation or illusory knowledge accepted as truth until the actuality of what is perceived is revealed.

1.12   The five activities of the mind can be brought into a state of Yoga through practice [an appropriate, accurate, focused and consistent one] and non-attachment [an active and committed disengagement with the diversions and distractions – the projections and preconceptions – that the ego defines itself by].

1.17   Perception [through the dedication and detachment that has created space for self-awareness] gradually becomes whole rather than disturbed by influences and impressions. A continued deepening of comprehension brings one into alignment with one's surroundings; with the joyous sense of "I am".

(Translation inspired by those of T. K. V. Desikachar and Swami Jnaneshvara Bharati)

"I am functioning, but I am not present," reads T. K. V. Desikachar's description in *The Heart of Yoga* of a chronically wavering attention, a symptom that has come to be a societal norm for those conditioned to do, want, and need more, faster and better. But the most disturbing part of this daily reality is that most would claim that they are barely *functioning* to begin with, going through the motions of a life dedicated to acquiring while in fact depriving themselves of the only one true thing to be had: the present moment. Fighting to stay afloat in a culture that values, applauds, and rewards resistance to this simple truth is a form of self-inflicted violence considering what one is settling for as a result: poor health, a bankrupt body, an insolvent mind, a broken spirit – a life of poverty. Actively choosing to victimize one's self – to function rather than flourish – is the definition of living unconsciously.

The compulsions of modernity do not permit respite: for the many who are desensitized to how familiar a fractured, fragmented way of being has become – day in, day out – the present moment has never felt so far away. Yet, as Louise Hay reminds us, "how you live your day is how you live your life." Imagine a day – let alone an entire lifetime – made up of present moments. This is precisely the promise of Yoga that Patanjali points to throughout the Sutras: healing, health, wellbeing, Wholeness; the realignment – Union – of our many layers of "self" through the practice of mindfulness.

"The temple bell stops/but the sound keeps coming out of the flowers," the Japanese haiku poet Basho once wrote – a reminder that, just like the temple bells, the benefits of Yoga do not stop when we step off of the mat or away from our practice; rather, as with the flowers, they continue to resonate within us. However, when we live by default – either because we have been convinced to pursue a certain lifestyle or because we are too exhausted to even consider the possibility of another – we are living a life not of mindfulness, but of misapprehension.

Misapprehension, as Patanjali warns us in Sutra 1.8, is a state of unconsciousness wherein one is influenced by or accepts false observation or illusory knowledge over the truth. When we are entrenched in and attached to a societal standard informed by false observation and illusory knowledge – by a "do, want, and need more, faster and better" approach to life – it is difficult to gain enough perspective to identify the truth: that such a way of being in the world demands more from us than can give us in return.

Arriving at this realization is either hopeless or hopeful – it points to no way out or the only way out. In both cases, we are confronted with the prospect that choosing happiness and Wholeness means giving up everything we have "invested" in: the "truths" of and consequential attachments to false observation and illusory knowledge that our identity has been founded upon. This understanding can be an alienating, disenchanting point of crisis, yet a crisis of health in body or mind can be just as much so. When we are "functioning but not present," it is simply a matter of which crisis reaches us first. In either case, however, a crisis may give us the distance, the perspective – the *opportunity* – for the *actuality of what is perceived to be revealed.*

As Patanjali points to throughout Sutras 1.2 – 1.17, when we see the truth for what it is, life unfolds: because we no longer give our energy to the projections, preconceptions, or preoccupations the ego had once assimilated itself with, we have access to a *place of clear and right perception.* Free from the world's diversions, disturbances, and distractions, we have the ability to redirect our minds without attachment to influences or impressions. This is the *joyous sense of* "I *am*" that realigns us with the present moment.

Because the quality of our lives is a reflection of the quality of our awareness, change, then, is only possible by becoming aware; when we are mindful of our options in regard to the behaviours we allow to inhabit/inhibit us and the choices we allow to direct/divert us, we are living consciously, presently. French theologian Nicolas Malebranche once observed that this state of mindfulness is, in fact, as innate to our being as the instincts that drive our survival; that, as he put it, "attentiveness is the natural prayer of the soul." Although the din of our multitasking, stimulating days and the tension, stress, and exhaustion that overwhelmingly comes with them seem to drown out this "prayer", it can be voiced again through yogic practices that help to develop our awareness.

Yogini Vanda Scaravelli once described this yoga process as a means of "purify[ing] the body and the mind bringing us back to that blessed state of receptivity from which we can start to learn." It is from this posture of mindfulness that we can "start to learn" how to live our lives as though at the "beginning", awakening to each day as a child: in a state of wonder and engagement without attachment, expectation, or influence. By encountering the world through the invocation of our "natural prayer" we rest

fully within the present moment, finding extension, growth, renewal, balance, consciousness, and connection again. As Patanjali points to, when we remain opened to the world with attentiveness, *the redirection of the mind without distraction* becomes effortless. *I am* becomes the everyday experience.

Grounding Reflections: Developing Awareness

~ In what ways am I "functioning but not present"? How are these ways stripping me of the present moment? Where, when, and with whom do I want to be fully present?

~ In what ways have I been "investing" in a "life of poverty"? What unfulfilling, toxic, or destructive thoughts and actions have compromised my physical, psychological, and spiritual wellbeing?

~ In what ways are my "investments" an imprint of a culturally accepted narrative of misapprehension – of false observations and illusory knowledge? What choices, behaviours, attitudes, motivations, desires, and ideals have I unconsciously adopted as my own living truth?

~ In what ways am I willing to surrender my sense of identity – the projections, preconceptions, and preoccupations of the ego – for the sense of "I am" – the pure perception of non-attachment that is free from influence and impression?

~ In what ways can I identify the quality of my life as

being directly related to the quality of my awareness? If the life I think I want has been distracting and diverting me away from the present moment, am I ready to accept that in order to change I must first become mindful of and attentive to the life I have?

Supporting Practices: Deepening Awareness

Asana – Tadasana (Mountain Pose):

Mountain Pose is a contemplative posture that brings us home to ourselves as we learn how to stand again. In *Tadasana* we give ourselves the time and space to become aware of our alignment and breath, to observe what is presenting itself to us in both the physical and emotional layers of the body, and to feel the integrity of standing with intention.

With feet hip-width distance apart, toes facing forward, take on a stance that allows you to feel present through all parts of each sole, creating a broad foundation. Scanning up the body, attentive to feedback and differences from side to side, track the knees over the ankles, the hips over the knees, the shoulders over the hips, and the ears over the shoulders. Supported by the earth beneath you, feel the weight of the body evenly distributed between the right and left foot, the backs of the knees unlocked, the hands at ease, and the shoulders relaxed back and down. If it is comfortable for you, close the eyes or let the gaze rest softly in front of you.

Invite the breath to be whole and nourishing, drawing the belly back subtly with each exhale to feel the midline lengthen, the spine both rising up while rooting down as the pelvis and crown spaciously stretch away from each other. Stand for ten breaths in this full bodymind awareness with the strength, dignity, and grace of a mountain, facing the elements while letting them pass as you reach for the blue sky beyond.

Extended Asana Practice:
Vrksasana (Tree Pose)
Parsvakonasana (Standing Side Stretch Pose)
Balasana (Child Pose)
Eka Pada Rajakapotasana (Royal Pigeon Pose)
Kumbhakasana/Vasisthasana (Plank Pose/Inclined Plane Pose)

Pranayama – Hara Breath (Deep-Belly Breath):
The *hara* is our energetic centre, located deep within the belly. It is the seat of our life force, our *prana*; a site charged with a vitality and inner awareness from which we can draw from, ground through, and replenish with

the breath.

Sitting in any comfortable position that allows the diaphragm, legs, and back to be at ease, become aware of your neutral breath and where it is showing itself in the body: is it strained, shallow, uneven, tense, painful, or is it free, full, smooth, loose, calm?

Closing the eyes, inhale through the nose and direct the breath down into the *hara* centre, allowing the belly to softly expand out as the lungs take on a full expression of themselves. Exhaling back out through the nose, gently draw the navel inwards, allowing the pelvis and sits bones to root down as the spine and diaphragm move up, pushing stale *prana* out from the *hara* and lower lobes while creating space within the body to receive fresh air and energy. Continue for ten long, intentional breaths, bringing conscious awareness back again and again to the wave-like movement in the rise and fall of the body as it radiates *prana* from within.

Dhyana – Mindful Eating:

Maintaining a *satvic* (or pure) diet of whole foods not only supports wellness, but can be very healing for disease and dis-ease in the body. Whenever possible, choose fresh, seasonal fruits and vegetables, a variety of whole grain and dairy products, seeds, nuts, ghee, and plant-based oils, natural sweeteners and juices, sweet, warming spices and teas, as well as coconut and filtered water.

Proper nutrition, however, is not the only part of a *satvic* approach to feeding ourselves consciously, for *how* we feed ourselves is an extension of our nourishment. Mindful eating asks of us to not only stay present with the aromas, tastes, colours, textures, and temperatures of our food, but with its source. Thich Nhat Hanh reminds us that "Each bite of food/contains the life of/the Sun and the Earth./The whole universe/ is in a piece of bread." To be a part of this process – the journey of time, conditions, and resources, both human and not – is a miracle, and eating mindfully is an expression of this awareness.

Let meal time, then, be an occasion for reverence and celebration: let go of distractions and be one with that which sustains you as an offering, an honouring. Slow down, breath, observe the senses and their evocations, and discover an entirely new – and vitally sustaining – experience of and relationship with both your food and that which you share with it: the present moment.

Setting Intentions: *Affirming Awareness*

I give myself wholly to the present moment
as an expression of gratitude for the only
one true thing that I have.

That which honours or heals me into Wholeness
receives the energy of my attention.

My true nature is one of pure perception
free from preconditions.

I think, act, and speak consciously
as an expression of my joyous living truth.
When I am aware, I *am* One.

~

~ Moving Inwards:
Meditations on Intention ~
Sutras 1.30-1.33:

1.30   *Nine obstacles that threaten to disturb one's journey towards reaching a state of Yoga include illness (physical and/or mental), inactivity (physical and/or mental), doubt (indecisiveness; distrust of self and/or others), ignorance (biased, misperceived, or incomplete comprehension), exhaustion (physical and/or mental), overindulgence (lack of self-discipline; compulsive, abusive, or addictive behaviours), delusion (inaccurate or self-serving projections and assumptions), apathy (lack of purpose), and instability (insecurity; tendency to regress).*

1.31   *These obstacles reveal themselves through symptoms that include disturbance and dis-ease in the body, mind, and breath.*

1.33   *By cultivating joy for those who have found happiness, compassion for those who suffer, benevolence towards those who are virtuous, and indifference towards those who act immorally, one's mind becomes purified and thus at ease.*

(Translation inspired by those of T. K. V. Desikachar and Swami Jnaneshvara Bharati)

~

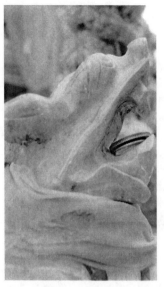

Living a life of intention requires us to acknowledge where we are displacing our energy. As Patanjali counsels us in Sutras 1.30 and 1.31, we can trace a depletion of personal resources to the presence in our lives of one or more of the nine obstacles and the all-consuming, manipulative, self-destructive way in which they demand authority over our energy. Illness, inactivity, doubt, ignorance, exhaustion, overindulgence, delusion, apathy, and instability oftentimes surface out of a lapse in self-regulation – in the ability to uphold our overall, long-term wellbeing by consciously aligning our actions with our deep-seated values. When we fail to focus our energies on nourishment, whether it be in the form of sleep, nutrition, bodymind health, service, fulfilling relationships, interests that bring joy, connection with nature, or time for stillness and silence, we give the nine obstacles a window of opportunity to stealthily take hold by simultaneously leeching from and contaminating our energetic anatomy.

When we give a barrier our power, it dilutes all other areas of life. Self-regulation collapses, as the values and actions that uphold our best interests become skewed or perhaps even unrecognizable. Consequentially, our capacity to filter and process physical and psychical intake becomes compromised, revealing what Patanjali describes as *symptoms that include disturbance and dis-ease in the body, mind, and breath.* These indicators may manifest as persistent fatigue, illness, migraines, and pain, or in feeling chronically distracted, reactive, anxious, irritable or depressed, among other states of disorder and dis-order.

Some of us live for so long in the chaos of displaced energy that we would not know who we are without it; it has come to define our way of engaging with and relating to the world and others. Internalizing a set of behaviours and outcomes that support our perceived mode of existence can become a vicious, damaging cycle, for we come to expect, attract, permit, engender, and sustain those same behaviours and outcomes. We lose all sense of intentionality in our lives.

"Do the best you can until you know better," advised the late poet Maya Angelou. "Then when you know better, do better." If illness, inactivity, doubt, ignorance, exhaustion, overindulgence, delusion, apathy, or instability has defined your terms of living, it is time to know better. You know better when you can identify where you have energetically misaligned your actions with your values. You do better when you start to live a life of intention.

Intentionality – or, more specifically, right-intention – arises out of the understanding that every thought, action, and word is an exchange of energy that either expends or expands our personal resources. As Patanjali attests, when we think, behave, and speak in accordance with values that nurture and protect our energy, the *mind becomes purified and thus at ease.* However, other people may not always think, behave, and speak in accordance with values that nurture and protect our energy; consequently, how we respond to these violations, transgressions, assaults, betrayals – whatever label one might give to them – is as equally important. Sutra 1.33 serves as a guideline to accessing a place of intentional living through creating, enriching, and attracting supportive energy that suppressive energy – whether our own or others' – cannot threaten.

When Patanjali challenges us to develop energetically sustainable attitudes towards the happiness, suffering, virtuousness, and immorality of others, he is also asking us to consider the ways in which we have held different standards for others than ourselves. Iyanla Vanzant, while quoting a friend in her book *One Day My Soul Just Opened Up*, puts it this way: "*When we judge what [others] have done, we are actually informing them of the conditions we place on loving them.*" Judgment, therefore, is a mechanism of fear, and the conditions we place on our love are an expression of that fear vying for control. When you measure your happiness against another's, fear gains control through envy; when your will to give compassionately hinges on the expectation of receiving something in return, fear gains control through animosity; when your own insecurities, comparisons, and self-criticisms threaten your ability to celebrate the virtuous lives of others, fear gains control through jealousy; and when you identify with being a victim of others' immorality, fear gains control through anger.

When the toxicity of judgment guides our relationships with other people – be they friends, family or strangers – we deflect back onto ourselves a reflection of its inherent fear, experiencing it in the proportionately toxic form of envy, animosity, jealousy, or anger. This "equal and opposite reaction" is rooted in the principle that all we energetically project into the world cannot be separated from us, and that our attempts to gain control through judgment and fear inevitably only strip it away. In the end, when we place conditions on our love for others, we are placing conditions on our love for ourselves.

One way of releasing these conditions is through the practice of non-judgment. When, to cite Chopra, we acknowledge that our lives are interconnected with every other life, the perceived desire "to oppose, resist, conquer, or destroy" falls away, for there is no need to control, no need to fear, no need to judge. Surrendering to this truth allows us to see ourselves in others, and for others to see themselves in us.

When you let go of the construct "other" for the experience of relating to people as extensions of yourself, your relationships become intentional. This comes with the understanding that envy, animosity, jealousy, and anger – the repercussions of fear – have as much of a negative impact on your energetic anatomy as they do on others. Alternatively, the energetically expansive and sustaining responses of non-judgment – joy, compassion, benevolence, and indifference – are beneficial to all, for they align thought, action, and word with right-intention. Thus, when we experience *joy for those who have found happiness*, we both receive and reflect the light of contentment; when we experience *compassion for those who suffer*, we divine from a reserve of kindness and empathy that is renewed the more it is shared from; when we experience *benevolence towards those who are virtuous*, we become nourished by the field of love and truth inherent in the good and in the mutual desire of good for all; and when we experience *indifference towards those who act immorally*, we cease to prop-up with our energy the unconscious, fear-based, ego-driven behaviours of others.

Intellectually, this last point is a difficult one to navigate around on our path to Union, especially given the atrocities human beings are capable of committing. In energetic terms, what Patanjali is asking us to do is see the person, not the behaviour. When we cease to judge others based on their behaviours, we choose instead to acknowledge the Higher Self within them – no matter how buried under one or more of the nine obstacles it may be. However, to humanize and make relatable those responsible for truly unspeakable behaviours, Vanzant encourages us to consider that *"People who commit those acts do so in fear, shame, or guilt. Is it wrong to be afraid or shamed, or to feel guilty?"* Furthermore, *"People do what they do based on who they are, what they believe, and the information they have at the time that supports their feelings and*

beliefs." Indifference, therefore, is not a dismissive act, but rather one that acknowledges the complexity of the human condition, as Vanzant speaks to, and the limits of placing upon it dualistic judgments. As the mystic Sufi poet Hafiz once counseled, "Now is the time to realize that all you do is sacred" – including your response to those who act on the profane.

"*You are not in the world;*" Chopra reminds us, "*the world is in you.*" When you think, behave, and speak in alignment with values that nourish and sustain both your energy and that of others, the world is within you; freed from fear, from judgement, from the influence of the nine obstacles, you become intentional. Right-intention places us within the context of love, and it is from within the context of love that, ultimately, the *mind becomes purified and thus at ease.*

Grounding Reflections: Developing Intention

~ In what ways can I establish one or more of the following nine obstacles as being either the result *of* or responsible *for* an inability to value my own wellbeing, or to think, act, and speak from a place of right intention:

~ physical and/or mental illness?

~ physical and/or mental inactivity?

~ doubt, indecisiveness, and/or distrust of self/others?

~ ignorance, bias, misperception, and/or incomplete comprehension?

~ physical and/or mental exhaustion?

~ overindulgence, lack of self-discipline, and/or compulsive, abusive, or addictive behaviours?

~ delusion and/or inaccurate/self-serving projections and assumptions?

~ apathy and/or lack of purpose?

~ instability, insecurity, and/or tendency to regress?

~ In what ways have one or more of the nine obstacles come to define how I relate to the world, to others, and to myself? Consequently, is there a recurring set of behaviours, outcomes, and experiences in my life that I unconsciously come to expect, attract, and create? What chronic symptoms of disorder or dis-order have arisen in my health – physically, mentally, emotionally, energetically – as a response? Who would I be without them?

~ In what ways am I willing to release my current perceived mode of existence in order to become this other potential self? Am I ready to surrender that which has defined my terms of living? Am I ready to commit to making every thought, action, and word an intentional exchange of energy in order to honour that of others and of myself?

~ In what ways have I held different standards for others than for myself? How is this reflected in one or more of the nine obstacles that I recognize as being dominant in my life?

~ In what ways have I withheld joy, compassion, benevolence, or indifference due to and overriding sense of envy, animosity, jealousy, or anger, respectively? Do I measure my happiness against that of others? Do I give compassion selflessly and without conditions? Do I feel threatened by the virtue of others due to my own insecurities? Do I self-identify as a victim in reaction to immoral behaviour?

~ In what ways has judgment falsely led me to see the behaviour, not the person? To see the behaviour, not my Self?

Supporting Practices: Deepening Intention

Asana – Supta Baddha Konasana (Reclining Bound Angle Pose):

In Reclining Bound Angle Pose we are invited to release the hips, pelvis, and chest as well as the stagnant tensions, emotions, and energies held within them that can stunt our capacity for intentionality and evolution.

Resting back with the knees bent and hip-width distance apart, place the soles of the feet on the ground and the hands over the *hara* centre. Feel your heavy pelvis draw you down as the elbows relax at your sides, the shoulder blades widen away from each other, and the head and neck decompress. Take a few deep, full, belly breaths here to allow the spine to lengthen as the low back releases towards the earth, letting go.

Walking the heels as high up towards the pelvis as is comfortable, place the soles of the feet together and gently drop the knees away from the midline as gravity slowly takes the legs towards the floor (supporting the knees with pillows, if necessary), freeing restrictions in and around your root centre. Notice how *Supta Baddha Konasana* takes you into a subtle backbend that expands the chest, welcoming the emotional body to reveal itself. As you open to this life-giving posture, observe without judgment or conditions; with the heart and hips reaching wide, let fear fall away and the fullness of love take its place.

After ten *hara* breaths, bring the knees back to together again and hug them towards the chest as the head and shoulders continue to rest back, feeling a joyous sense of spaciousness in the body where there once was holding.

Extended Asana Practice
Adho Mukha Svanasana (Downward Facing Dog Pose)
Setu Bandhasana (Bridge Pose)
Utkatasana (Chair Pose)
Bhujangasana (Cobra Pose)
Ardha Matsyendrasana (Seated Half Spinal Twist Pose)

Pranayama – Brahmari (Bee Breath):

Brahmari is the Sanskrit word for bee, and in this breathwork named after the insect's humming wings we discover just how profoundly healing sound and its resonance can be. As it teases out emotional and energetic blockages in the body, relaxes the breath, calms the mind, and eases the nervous system, *brahmari* is an intentional practice that nourishes intentionality, expanding *prana* where it has otherwise been expended.

Sitting comfortably, become attentive to how the presence of one or more of the nine obstacles – of illness, inactivity, doubt, ignorance, exhaustion, overindulgence, delusion, apathy, or instability – may be asserting itself on your natural breath by way of a sense of fear, heaviness, or withholding in the chest. Stay with these sensations, just observing.

When you are ready, close the eyes and inhale fully through the nose into the low belly. Keeping the lips softly sealed, exhale slowly while allowing the out-breath to take on a deep humming sound at heart centre. Feel the pelvis ground as the spine soars upwards by drawing the navel back gently as you hum.

Continue for ten or more long breaths, noticing how the whole being loosens and lets go in response to the soothing vibration within, carrying with it a radiating sense of wellbeing. Feel how this place gives you the presence to create change, to choose joy, compassion, benevolence, and indifference – to live with intention.

Dhyana – Metta Prayer (Loving-Kindness Meditation):

Loving-Kindness is a transformative practice that shifts us from seeing every person as a catalogue of behaviours to accepting all beings as individual expressions of consciousness, with some more present than others. Though behaviour is defined by awareness, it is not wrong for someone to be more or less aware than another; thus, the *Metta* Prayer can become an equalizer – a means for understanding those we have found difficult to relate to, or whose actions have been challenging to forgive. Loving-Kindness empowers us, then, through the reframing of who and what receives our energy, and of why and how we give it.

In our *Metta* practice, we internally chant the following phrases:

May I be free from danger.
May I be happy.
May I be healthy.
May I be at ease.

After several repetitions, we direct our meditation towards three others – a family member, friend, or mentor, a stranger or neutral person, and an individual we have a strained, hostile, or estranged relationship with. Lastly, we finish by sending Loving-Kindness to all living beings.

Be intentional with this practice: sit with intention, chant with intent. Make yourself – your generosity, your gratitude, your graciousness – available to the world, to the desire for the greater good of all, and watch as you become liberated from withholding by the return of intentionality rushing back to you.

Setting Intentions: Affirming Intention

I choose what I give my power to.

I live with right-intention;
I do not place conditions on my
joy, compassion, benevolence, or indifference.

I expect, attract, permit, create, and sustain nourishing
behaviours, influences, and outcomes that both
expand and protect my energy and that of others.

The world is an extension of myself;
I do not hold different standards for others
than I do for myself.

I see the person, not the behaviour.

My non-judgment releases me from fear,
allowing me to see myself in others, and for others to
see themselves in me.

~

Pitta Season

Pitta is the "season" of early adulthood in the Ayurvedic lifecycle, a time of ambition, affirmation, and establishment. We, too, now enter the Pitta Season of our Yogic Path, confronting such pitta imbalances as compulsion and control while cultivating the pitta qualities of introspection and will through the practices of purpose and surrender.

~ Moving Inwards: Meditations on Purpose ~
Sutras 1.36-1.47:

1.36 *[When difficulty arises, interrupting the path to Union], clarity and serenity can be restored through meditation on the limitless, luminous light within.*

1.39 *Inquiry is meditation for the mind; it redirects and focuses thought, bringing it back home to a state of tranquility.*

1.43 *Through immersed inquiry one becomes freed from the conditioning of previous experiences, allowing distortions and distractions to fall away. The mind becomes transparent and open; rather than being susceptible to influences and impressions, it takes on a crystalline quality, reflecting the inquired. The perceiver and the perceived are one as pure perception.*

1.47 *It is through this Yogic state that one begins to cultivate true consciousness of self and a deep-seated understanding of one's very being.*

(Translation inspired by those of T. K. V. Desikachar and
Swami Jnaneshvara Bharati)

~

Purpose is the knowingness behind intention – the "I am" of what Patanjali describes as the *limitless, luminous light within.* However, becoming aware of the "I am" also means becoming aware of the "I am not". Modernity and its culture of self-promotion has manipulated the world into affiliating many things with a sense of "I am", but you are not your titles and talents, your credits and celebrity, your account balance and the possessions that project it, your social media status, your body and how you use, dress, or measure it, your diagnosis or disorder, your relationships and associations, your attitudes and ambitions. These self-concepts and schemas (which, arguably, are the difficulties Patanjali speaks of in Sutra 1.36 that interrupt one's path to Union) may piece together our identity, but purpose is not synonymous with identity – with what you have attached yourself to. This is because identity is based upon the circumstances and consequences you live under – the temporal, the topical – and is therefore comprised of that which can be striped away from you. As the Sutras point to, identity is thus not *true consciousness of self*, but the *conditioning of previous experiences*. An authentic sense of "I am" is not limited to or by these experiences; rather, as Patanjali assures us, an authentic sense of "I am" is limit-*less*. You cannot be striped of your limitlessness.

What, then, is this *limitless, luminous light*? The "I am" – *true consciousness of self*. And what is *self*? *Clarity, serenity, tranquility, transparency* and *openness* – our true nature. What is our purpose? *Pure perception*: to *reflect* the truth of reality rather than that which *distorts, distracts, influences,* and *impresses* upon it. How do we achieve this state of being? By *redirecting and focusing thought* through *meditation*; through *inquiry*.

Inquiry is the mindful monitoring of content that enters and occupies consciousness; it reflects an understanding of how crucial the condition of one's mindscape is to a sense of wholeness and wellbeing, and signals a commitment to changing and maintaining the quality of one's inner climate. Yet, in order for inquiry to take on this act of self-healing, it must come from a place free from judgement and criticism, a place infused with the resolve to gain perspective on perspective through patience and compassion – a place in which, despite what may be revealed, one is willing to love one's self. This place is the witness within, wherein, rather than engaging with that which presents itself to us, we observe its effects instead. This practice has the power to enable profound inner shifts to take place: old, cyclical routines and monologues within the bodymind begin to loosen their grip, and a sense of spaciousness starts to get teased out from between our hardened knots of thought. It is from within this parting, this distance created between "thought" and "I am", that one is given a glimpse into what Patanjali writes is our one true purpose – to experience the world through pure perception; then, the questions follow: How does this thought or idea serve me? How does this behaviour or emotion serve me? How does this form of communication or expression serve me? How does this action or task serve me? How does this need or want serve me? Does it serve my conditioning, or does it serve my awakening? What is its purpose to me, and how does it serve my purpose?

Assessing rather than attaching to one's thoughts is an innate ability to us all, but it cannot be cultivated without taking time to be present with them. When we do, accessing that realm of stillness, of "no-mind", that is ever-available for us to step back into and watch ourselves from, we gain greater autonomy within the mind – "a higher vantage point," as spiritual teacher Eckhart Tolle might say, "from which to view the events in your life instead of being trapped inside them." Essentially, we start to deconstruct our self-image by actively disidentifying with what Tolle terms as "object consciousness": the dependency on transient "objects" ("material things, things to do, [and] things to think about") as qualifiers of a sense of "I am", of purpose. The unreal separates from the real, and our inquiry begins to move deeper: How does my guilt or grief serve my purpose or that of others? How does my denial or resistance serve my purpose or that of others? How does my suffering or victimhood serve my purpose or that of others? My bias, intolerance, or rejection? My vanity, pride or conceit? How does my contempt, hostility, or spite serve my purpose or that of others? My impatience? My unaccountability? My anxiety, distrust or cynicism? How does my greed, manipulation, or competitiveness serve my purpose or that of others? How does my rigidity or unwillingness to forgive serve my purpose or that of others?

These inward-looking questions mobilize us into new behaviour patterns for, when we surrender pretence, face our own conditioning, and take responsibility for any role we may have played in creating or perpetuating our own suffering, we begin to understand the nature of the self-narrative we have been investing in. This narrative is the scripting of our internal dialogues - the parasitic, compulsive, or negatively self-fulfilling thoughts, emotions, and behaviours that have come to shape our ideas about who we are, and thus the world around us. Without inquiry, the more we come to identify with these dialogues, the more we come to believe them, and the more we believe them, the more we seek to reaffirm them. Reaffirmation can take the form of skewed expectations, a non-receptivity to the reality you experience outside of those expectations, a manipulation or sabotaging of the reality you experience, or a narrow, stagnant outlook in which you only see what you choose to see. According to Tolle, this is the "pain-body" (or an "addiction to unhappiness") at work, seeking to sustain emotional negativity by controlling your thoughts and attracting compatible energy in others. The power of inquiry is that it equips us with what Patanjali refers to as a form of meditation; by virtue of becoming aware of these dialogues we are empowered to objectively navigate instead of passively internalize them. Essentially, we become a host to rather than a product of our thoughts.

This quality of mindfulness is at the very marrow of becoming conscious of our consciousness, of pursuing our true purpose. To quote from writer Robert Byrne, "the purpose of life is a life of purpose" – a life, Patanjali might respond, in which the mind *takes on a crystalline quality, reflecting the inquired.* The

inquired, therefore, is really that which exists "out there" that causes a response "in here"; when we inquire into that response, we shed the viral tendency of thought for an untampered expression of the "out there" that is now "in here". When there is no separation between the within and the without, *the perceiver and the perceived are one as pure perception. It is through this Yogic state*, Patanjali writes, *that one begins to cultivate true consciousness of self and a deep-seated understanding of one's very being*: that we are not our thoughts, but the awareness behind them. Through questioning the *perceiver* we come to know the *perceived*, and together they make the "I am": pure perception – the experience of experience itself. Once we begin, inquiry becomes no less than a way of life, a way of *purpose*.

Grounding Reflections: Developing Purpose

~ In what ways have I been conditioned into identifying my material existence in the world as synonymous with my purpose in life; with my sense of "I am"?

~ In what ways have my thoughts, ideas, behaviours, emotions, forms of communication and expression, actions, tasks, needs, and wants continued to serve this conditioning rather than my purpose? How are my habitual ways of being purposeful to me? How do they serve my purpose?

~ In what ways have my internal dialogues determined my suffering and consequently my experience of the world and others? How have these experiences further reaffirmed my self-narrative?

Supporting Practices: Deepening Purpose

Asana – Virabhadrasana (Warrior Pose):

Warrior is a balancing pose that asks of us to be fully committed to its purpose: to align, ground, engage, connect, lengthen, and focus the many layers of Self in an affirming stance that builds stability and stamina in both the muscles and the mind. By making ourselves available to *Virabhadrasana* as a full-body inquiry, staying present with the posture, we permit ourselves the room to step back into and observe from as we occupy a deeper inner landscape of consciousness.

Return to your Mountain Pose practice, taking the time to arrive in the stance, in the breath. On an exhalation, bring the palms of the hands together at heart centre in *Namaste*. On your next out-breath, drop the arms down along your sides and take a straight stride back with the right foot so that the feet remain hip-width distance apart, toes facing forward. Lift the left toes up to feel a firm foundation root you down through the right heel, then lower the toes as you bend the front knee so that it is stacked over top of the ankle joint below it, keeping the back leg extended and its foot fully present on the ground. With the hips and shoulders squared off, exhale and reach the arms up overhead, encouraging them to align alongside the ears. Shrug the shoulders down, face the palms towards one another, and lengthen through the fingertips. With eyes softly focused on a point in front of you, feel the heavy pelvis ground you through your strong legs as the spine rises upwards with the crown of the head. Let go of any rigidity and become aware of a sense of lightness, of limitlessness – that you are not supporting the pose, but that the pose is supporting you.

After ten whole, relaxed breaths, lower the arms as you step back into *Tadasana*, finishing with *Namaste* before repeating on the other side, leading with the left foot. As you move through your Warrior practice, stay with what presents itself to you – physically, emotionally, energetically, spiritually – with loving non-judgment. As you open into what yogini Vanda Scaravelli coined as "the song of the body," experience *Virabhadrasana* as an expression of knowingness – as a luminous entry-point into perspective and purpose.

Extended Asana Practice
Salabhasana (Locust Pose)
Trikonasana (Triangle Pose)
Garudasana (Eagle Pose)
Urdhva Mukha Svanasana (Upward Facing Dog Pose)
Navasana (Boat Pose)

Pranayama & Dhyana – Tantric Space
Meditation:

Tantric practices are the "Yoga of energy,"
and in the two-part Space Meditation that
transitions *pranayama* into *dhyana* we use our
present moment experiences as a form of
inquiry into how the mind displaces and
reclaims this energy. Thought cannot exist
without space around which it can form into;
thus, the mind's predisposed state is not one of
overcrowding but of stillness, silence. This is the
"I am" of Self, the crucible of pure perception.

Sit with ease, the spine straight but the body
soft, and bring your attention to the *Ajna*
Chakra – the Third-Eye point at the centre of
the brow that connects us with our intuition,
insight, and innate wisdom. Loosen the belly
and invite the breath to be smooth and whole as
you become aware of the natural pause that fills
the space between each inhale and exhale. Do
not attach to or affect this opening, only
witness it.

After several minutes with the breath, slowly
shift your focus to the same natural pause that

fills the space between each thought. Rather than engaging with impressions and talking back to voices that appear and reappear – a futile outsourcing of energy that only draws from and depletes other areas of the body – gesture your awareness around and beyond the thoughts as they pass through consciousness. Maintaining the inward gaze of the Third-Eye, abide in this birthright to quietude as all else simply falls away, leaving the Buddha Within.

Setting Intentions: Affirming Purpose:

"I am" not limited to or by my experiences,
within or without,
because "I am" an expression of the limit-less.

"I am" a witness; I step back into the
loving-healing of stillness
and assess rather than attach to that which I observe.

Inquiry creates change; when "I am" aware of
that which enters consciousness,
I allow in only that which is purposeful to my purpose.

"I am" not my thoughts,
but the knowingness behind them.

My light is self, my self is purpose, my purpose is perception, my perception is pure; "I am" both the perceiver and the perceived.

~

~ Moving Inwards:
Meditations on Surrender ~
Sutras 2.5-2.20:

2.5   Ignorance (avidya) [which is the source of egoism, attachment, aversion, and insecurity] leads to the internalization of the unreal for the real.

2.6   Egoism (asmita) is identification with thought as source of self and perception.

2.7   Attachment (raga) is based in the conviction that material attainment is synonymous with happiness.

2.8   Aversion (dvesa) is the result of past experiences of suffering being associated with specific circumstances or objects, whether they still exist or not.

2.9   Insecurity (abhinivesah) – an affliction of both the innocent and the wise – is the toxic, often irrational energy that is fuelled by an anxiety in the unknowable; in what lies ahead.

2.17 Suffering arises from actions [which are influenced by the obstacles of egoism, attachment, aversion, and insecurity] that stem from the inability to differentiate the perceived (or object) from the perceiver (or subject).
2.20 The subject is the witnessing consciousness; however, this perceiver sees through the lens of the mind. Thus, one's quality of perception is subject to the state of one's mind; is affected by the lens that lies between the subject and the object, the perceiver and that which is being perceived.

(Translation inspired by those of T. K. V. Desikachar and Swami Jnaneshvara Bharati)

~

When we become clear about our purpose to fulfill our true nature – witnessing consciousness – we begin the process of shedding living as a victim of thought for living as a student of awareness. This transition demands that we confront the self-narratives revealed to us through inquiry by accepting that that which is born out of *the internalization of the unreal for the real* cannot support growth; cannot allow space for evolution. Our past thoughts, emotions, and behaviours – all projections of our ingrained conditioning and thus misperception of reality – suddenly no longer align with what we now know about and want for ourselves. And yet, the question remains: What are we *really* willing to do about it?

Through the distance of inquiry, some of us, in

stepping back enough to truly *hear* what we think and *see* how we act, may be mortified beyond response by that which we find within, our inner life seeming too maniacal, disturbing, unforgiveable – unsalvageable. In fact, we may walk away from inquiry with the self-deprecating conviction that we are positively unlovable because of what we think, and the ways in which we have allowed this to colour *the lens of the mind* and therefore our discouraging experience of the world. Inquiry may also have pointed us back towards the trauma, pain, or vulnerability of our first encounters with what we later came to believe about ourselves. These encounters – no matter what shape they took, no matter who they came from – are parasites of one of the highest forms of violation against the spirit and abuses of human consciousness: devaluation. Devaluation never marks just one life, but brands the immediate lives of others with the potential to bleed through many generations. Inquiry might seem a cruel provoker when bringing one to the task of revisiting the past in order to deconstruct the present. Or perhaps inquiry has caught us off guard with two impossible possibilities: to fly in the face of the only reality we have ever known by destabilizing the self-images we have painstakingly constructed for ourselves, or to turn around and walk away from the necessity to change with the knowledge that you had the opportunity, the *reason*, to do so.

Awareness is not passive; if we want *the lens of the mind* to stop failing us with *the internalization of the unreal for the real*, then we must act on what has been exposed by inquiry. As Patanjali would argue, all of the above responses to this exposure are rooted in different mechanisms of that which obscures knowledge (*avidya*): egoism, attachment, aversion, and insecurity. Though these obstacles differ in character, they all affect right-perception in the same way by tampering with our ability to *differentiate the perceived (or object) from the perceiver (or subject)*. What

Patanjali is commenting on here is that suffering is a consequence of the absence of knowingness – of the experience that we are not separate from that which we perceive, but one with it. It is easy to demonize egoism, attachment, aversion, and insecurity for this deprivation and betrayal, but we must choose to believe that they ultimately have the potential to lead us to a higher place; that their purpose to us is not to consume but to counter in order that we may know all that it is possible for us to be. "Balance comes from experiencing all dimensions of life," Osho encourages us, for it is only through that which forces us to acknowledge the truth about ourselves that we are able to move deeper.

"Happiness," Osho goes on to say, "is egolessness" – is a surrendering of the misery that makes us "special". However, the ego is none too eager to relinquish the constructs it has created in order to reaffirm itself to itself; without the storied identity the ego uses to draw attention to and define itself by, it cannot thrive and survive. For this reason, the ego is referred to in Sanskrit as *ahamkara*, the "I maker" – that part of ourselves driven to *identif[y] with thought as source of self*. Our current culture of narcissism, competition, and self-promotion is a product of this delusion; we *live* in the age of the "I maker", in the arena of the ego. Everywhere we turn the ego has given itself ample opportunity to indulge and applaud itself by standing in place of reality. But why this desperation, this compulsion to assert existence? Because the ego – like insecurity, aversion, and attachment – functions from a place of fear.

"Fear is a distraction from 'what is', from the present moment, preventing us from existing, from being what we are," wrote Vanda Scaravelli in her luminous book *Awakening the Spine*. As a result, Scaravelli explains, "We are always in a hurry, we run, we run, we run, in order to be able to do as many things as possible: to achieve, to become, to obtain. To run is a symptom of fear, to run after something, after somebody. We are slaves not only to others, but to ourselves, to our ideas, to our ambitions, to our projects, and even to our mental projections. This is a miserable attitude that life does not deserve." Our running, then, is a mechanism of fear, of the ego's restlessness to both grasp at and resist that which it cannot control. In an attempt to "run after" or materialize the self (which, by virtue, is both separate and therefore false), we pad our lives up with "distractions", narratives: with things (attachment), with the past (aversion), with the future (insecurity) – with that which is founded in and consequently only valuable to thought (ego).

So how does one begin the process of stripping away this separate, false self-story? What sieve, as Scaravelli might ask, must one hold out under life "through which superficial things drop away leaving only what is essential"? How *do* we align with what we now know about and want for ourselves? In order to let go of the bodymind's disease and dis-ease we must be willing to surrender. Surrender the answer to the question "Who am I?" – it is merely conditional on the ego's perception of the present, on the *unreal*. Surrender the fiction of controlling the unknowable – it is not the same as knowingness. Surrender the life you have created – it is not the life you have.

When we surrender, we release fear by accepting vulnerability. However, being vulnerable does not mean being weak; it means trusting in the process of life – an act of deep-seated strength. To be vulnerable means to courageously rest in the truth of "what is" with the conviction that it is riskier to live with a heart protected by pretense than with one laid bare to the world. To be open and receptive is to be sensitive, and to be sensitive is to love, and love, as Zen Master Nissim Amon assures us, is "the one thing that can overcome fear."

Grounding Reflections: Developing the
Ability to Surrender

~ In what ways do my past thoughts, emotions, and behaviours no longer align with what I now know about and want for myself?

~ In what ways have I experienced devaluation in my life, either from my self or others? How has this come to shape what I believe about myself?

~ In what ways are mechanisms of fear – egoism, attachment, aversion, insecurity – standing in place of reality in my life?

~ In what ways am I willing to surrender my constructs and control in order to trust in and be vulnerable to the process of life?

Supporting Practices: Deepening the Ability to Surrender

Asana – Pranatasana (Mouse Pose):

When we come into Mouse Pose, we take on the shape of a fetal position. Though we often think of new life as vulnerable, its survival hinges of what seems like an unfathomable strength: to surrender; to trust that it will breathe when it's supposed to breathe, to grow when it's supposed to grow. This utter relinquishment of control in order to give oneself wholly over to the process of life is therefore a birthright to us all; it is alive within us by virtue of being alive, and thus available to us in the face of fear.

Kneeling on a comfortable surface, sit your pelvis back towards your heels, placing a pillow behind the knees if needed. With the shins and tops of the feet rooting into the earth, fold forward over the upper thighs, taking the knees wider apart to create space for the front of the body if necessary. Allow the forehead to rest on the ground in front of the knees as you stretch the arms straight out in front of you, lowering the elbows down onto the floor when you are ready. If the forehead cannot reach the surface beneath you without the pelvis coming up from the heels, stack the fists one over the other and gently place the brow on top.

With each inhalation, invite the breath into the low belly, feeling the body rise as the ribcage expands, creating space between the shoulder blades. As you draw the navel back at the end of every exhale, notice the tailbone dropping farther down towards the heels as the body releases, allowing the spine to let go of compression and lengthen up through the resting head. Add a realigning rotation for the spine and opener for the thoracic area by looping the right arm under the left and turning the head (which continues to rest on the ground, or on a pillow if it cannot make contact) to look out over the right palm as it faces upwards. Repeat on the other side as you continue your breathing before returning back to neutral *Pranatasana*. Experience how Mouse

Pose eases the nervous system in response to its forward bend, regulating, calming, and grounding the bodymind as a result.

As the name suggests, *Pranatasana* is a *pranic* practice; as we bow down around and embrace our energetic core – the Solar Plexus, the seat of vitality – we become intimately familiar with this centre as both a sustainer and a messenger. Be at ease in this place; listen to your knowingness. Give yourself permission to surrender trauma; by this resolve, you will also be giving yourself permission to welcome peace.

Extended Asana Practice
Matsyasana (Fish Pose [Supported or Non-Supported])
Malasana (Garland Pose)
Parsvottanasana (Single Leg Forward Bend Pose)
Parighasana (Gate Pose)
Parivrtta Sukhasana (Revolved Easy Pose)

Pranayama – Hatha Sweeping Breath:
Like the broom that sweeps the floors in the temple of an ashram, this restorative *pranayama* practice is designed to clear away clutter in the

temple of the body.

Coming into a standing or supine position (outdoors in the healing palm of nature whenever possible), become aware of the layer of sediment left behind by disease and dis-ease: toxic emotions, residues of pain, dust from old, worn-out narratives. On an inhale, sweep the body with the breath as it enters through the soles of the feet, moving all the way up to the crown of the head. As you exhale, allow the breath to sweep back down and out the soles of the feet, purifying the body as it takes with it anything that no longer supports what you now know about and want for yourself.

Continue at your own pace for several repetitions, drawing in the breath as you welcome the abundance and blessings you have created space for, and exhaling as you surrender the egoism, attachment, aversion, and insecurity that has withheld your limitlessness from you.

Dhyana – Soham Mantra ("I am That" Mantra):

Sanskrit is considered to represent the primordial sound – the vibrational language of the Universe that is common to us all. Dating back thousands of years to the *Vedic* period, *mantras* were originally designed around the healing properties of certain syllables and how, when chanted either alone or together, these utterances could generate transformative psycho-physical benefits. Traditionally, each *mantra* is repeated in *Sanskrit* one-hundred-and-eight times, the auspicious number of repetitions believed to move one deeply into the *mantra* as a form of meditation and have the *nadis* (or energy channels in the body) respond to its resonance. As with all *mantras*, the *Soham* meditation is centred on a specific invocation or evocation – a phrase, affirmation, salutation, blessing, intention, or invitation; it this case we chant, either internally or audibly, "I am That" – "That" referring to witnessing consciousness, to our true nature.

Sitting and breathing as in the *hara* practice, inhale into the low belly while repeating "So" (mentally or softly under the breath), and exhale fully, chanting "*ham*" (pronounced "hum", done in the same way as you did "So"), observing how the *mantra* mimics the sound of the air-flow as it enters and leaves the body. Continue at your own pace, with intention, smoothing out the breath as the mind becomes one-pointed, as the body carries the *mantra* within it. Surrender; let all else simply fall away. The only self-story you need is the one without words, the one with only sound: "I am That"; *Soham*.

Setting Intentions: Affirming the Ability to Surrender

I surrender my answers to the question "Who am I?" –
they are merely conditional on, and consequently
only valuable to, the ego's perception and
projection of the unreal.

I surrender to the understanding that
there is nothing to lose but the unreal itself.

I surrender the fiction of controlling the unknowable –
it is not the same as experiencing knowingness,
the one truth of "what is".

I surrender the life I have created for the life I have –
for all that it is possible for me to be.

I surrender the contraction of fear
for the expansion of love.

~

Vata Season

Vata, in the *Ayurvedic* cycle of life, is the "season" of late adulthood, a time of expansion and liberation. The *Vata Season* of our Yogic Path is one in which we address such *vata* imbalances as ungroundedness and anxiety while we deepen the *vata* qualities of clarity and connection through healing transformation and Universal Consciousness.

~ Moving Inwards:
Meditations on Healing ~
Sutras 2.29-2.32:

2.29   *The eight limbs of Yoga include guidelines regarding one's relationships with others (yama) and with the self (niyama), the practice of Yoga postures (asana), the practice of breathing techniques (pranayama), withdrawing the senses to move inwards (pratyahara), mindfulness (dharaha), meditation (dhyana), and oneness (samadhi).*

2.30   *Yama is comprised of non-harm towards all living things (ahimsa), truthful communication (satya), non-covetousness (asteya), moderation of energetic resources (brahmacharya), and non-attachment (aparigrahah).*

2.32   *Niyama is comprised of purity (sauca), contentment (santosha), self-discipline (tapas), self-study (svadhyaya), and surrender to the Divine (Isvara Pranidhana).*
      (Translation inspired by those of T. K. V. Desikachar
                  and Swami Jnaneshvara Bharati)

~

Surrender is an invocation for self-healing, and self-healing is an expression of choice. Like water running over the rock of a riverbed, it is hard to reroute the mind from the channels, grooves, and trenches it finds the comfort of pattern and routine in. Ultimately, however, *we* act anchored in the understanding that there is nothing to lose in life but the unreal itself. Patanjali's eight limbs of Yoga serve as a map for choosing change on our journey towards living a life of union. As a Buddhist proverb reads, "Thoughts become words. Words become actions. Actions become habits. Habits become character. Watch your character,/For it becomes your destiny." When we "watch our character" from a place of intention that is nourished and informed by the practices of Yoga, we start to re-chart our destiny; we start to heal. As living externally falls away, our thoughts, words, actions, and habits begin to reflect a life lived from within.

Perhaps most integral to our healing is the practice of *ahimsa* – non-harm. Consciously choosing to ground thought, action, and speech in the desire to do no harm, injury, or violence to another being is an invitation for peace. As writer and visionary Duane Elgin explains in *Voluntary Simplicity*, "We cannot expect there to be peace within the human family if we are at war within ourselves." Letting go of the "war" within – the hostility, the fear, the trappings of the ego – is therefore a gesture of peace; because *ahimsa* is an equalizer, we no longer pose as a threat to ourselves, *or* to others. Practicing non-harm towards others is thus a way of practicing non-harm towards ourselves; of "caring for ourselves enough to forgive people," *including* ourselves, as mystic Caroline Myss attests, so that we may divest in the "marketing" and "authority" of our pain, our storytelling, our thoughts – our "war".

Once we start to view all other lives as interconnected with the experience of our own, we cannot help but consider the consequence of our choices – of our "character" – prayerfully. It is in this way that non-harm is also a way in which to receive and respond to the world; knowing the weight of our conduct, our every movement – whether of body or mind – takes on the quality of a devotional; becomes an expression of gratitude, wonder, reverence, love, healing.

Ahimsa is an offering; to accept is to walk the gentle path with complete conviction that non-harm is all the armor one will ever need. From a posture of non-harm, all other facets of Patanjali's eight-limbed path to union not only become possible, but transformative – particularly the *yamas* and *niyamas*:

~ Truthful Communication (*Satya*): Any form other than honest speech has the potential to create harm. *Ahimsa* encompasses *satya* through conscious speech – through practicing what, when, and how to speak the truth with loving-kindness and intention.

~ Non-Covetousness (*Asteya*): Regardless of whether your purpose is to hurt or not, stealing possessions, time, space (physical and sensory), or energy (physical and emotional) is the taking of something that is not yours to take. *Asteya* and *ahimsa* unite through the act of discerning how to have what is rightfully available to you without hindering or harming yourself or others – be they people, animals, or natural resources.

~ Moderation of Energetic Resources (*Brahmacharya*): Displacing or depleting our energy is a form of abuse, and where there is abuse of power – whether towards one's self or within other relationships – there is an absence of non-harm. Practicing *brahmacharya* thus means practicing *ahimsa*; by reserving our energy from that which in effect lays waste our resources we honour the limits and boundaries of ourselves and others.

~ Non-Attachment (*Aparigrahah*): Permanence is an illusion: it cannot be held on to or controlled. Identifying with or attaching to that which is ultimately transient – people, places, things – can only create harm through the pain and disenchantment one experiences in their inevitable loss. Letting go of possessiveness so that we may rest in "what is" aligns us with the present through the *ahimsa* of *aparigrahah*.

~ Purity (*Sauca*): The idiom "cleanliness is next to Godliness" is one way of defining both *ahimsa* and *sauca*, for when we are pure in body and mind, we are closest to our Highest Self. When the treatment of our bodies and thoughts, actions, and words reflect this understanding, we are practicing non-harm through purity.

~ Contentment (*Santosha*): Because contentment is an internal rather than external resource, we can never experience joy and ease if we are treating our physical, emotional, or spiritual selves in destructive ways. True *santosha* starts first with *ahimsa*.

~ Self-Discipline (*Tapas*): Yoga requires of us a commitment to mindful living, so that our every choice is a conscious reflection of this intention. *Tapas* is a guide through this process as it encourages us to pause in order to consider whether what we are engaging with is a nourishing or healing act for ourselves and others. If it is not, then it does not belong on our Yogic Path. The decisiveness of *tapas* necessitates a patience with and kindness towards ourselves that only *ahimsa* can make a possibility.

~ Self-Study (*Svadhyaya*): Confronting ourselves by looking inwards is one of the most difficult things we are called upon to do for Union – an act that cannot be broached unless, from a place of non-harm, we first decide that we value ourselves enough to do so. We must be willing to learn from and courageously accept the expansiveness that comes from the conviction that, to quote Myss, "Each of life's challenges is a lesson in some aspect of love." It is through *ahimsa* that *svadhyaya* is made possible.

~ Surrender to the Divine (*Isvara Pranidhana*):

Because, as Myss affirms, all lessons are born of love, it follows that the source of these lessons and the realm within which they are presented to us must also be a reflection of this love. When we open ourselves to experiencing our lives as love in action, we discover our true essence; we find the Divine. This surrender allows us to reframe encounters with pain and suffering not as challenges that inflicted harm but that forged a channel to our highest spiritual selves. Knowing this, we ground in Love – in the *ahimsa* of *Isvara Pranidhana*.

As the world becomes an extension of our self-healing and, subsequently, our transformation, the everyday becomes an opportunity to "place one stone on another," according to the sage yogi T. K. V. Desikachar – an endeavor in which we address past "residue[s] left behind by... action" by creating new ones that constructively influence those that follow. *Avidya* – the cloudiness of egoism, attachment, aversion, and insecurity that Desikachar describes as the "the root cause of the obstacles that prevent us from recognizing things as they really are" – falls away, and we are left with a life yet unlived.

The riverbed lies before us, smooth; destiny
awaits.

Grounding Reflections: Developing the Capacity for Healing

~ In what ways have I identified my pain and suffering – my "war" – as irrevocably who I am? Do I find comfort in the familiarity of holding on to this storyline? Am I willing to give it up?

~ In what ways am I ready to make self-healing an active, daily choice? Am I prepared for the work, effort, and change required of me to self-heal? Am I afraid of failing at healing, of the process, or of the stranger I might seem to myself and others afterwards?

~ In what ways do I envision my world – my destiny – transformed through my self-healing? If this transformation means losing all that is unreal in my life, am I willing to face what the unreal will prove to be?

~ In what ways have I knowingly or unknowingly created harm in my life or the lives of others? How will committing to grounding my thoughts, actions, speech, habits – my character – in the desire to do no harm, injury, or violence to myself or others invite peace, healing, and transformation into my life?

Supporting Practices: Deepening the Capacity for Healing

Asana – Viparita Karani (Supported Half Shoulder Stand):

In this variation of *Viparita Karani* we use a wall to support our legs so that there is no effort in the body, making it an entirely restorative posture – an intentional act of non-harm towards ourselves that gestures to the understanding that a therapeutic practice is as beneficial as a dynamic one.

Sit on a blanket, towel, or mat that has had its short edge lined up along the base of a wall.

Press your left hip against the wall and swing the legs up as you recline backwards, repositioning yourself as needed so that the seat and backs of the legs are making as much contact with the wall as possible. Separate the legs to hip-width distance apart, place the hands on the *hara* centre, and lie back with ease as you breathe wholly, feeling the lumbar spine ground down towards the earth as it loosens its tensions.

Continue on in Supported Half Shoulder Stand for ten or more breaths, noticing how the inversion of this full-body *mudra* begins to shift your physical and emotional energy: tired or swollen legs and feet begin to find relief; the breath and heart-rate centre themselves as the nervous system decompresses, promoting proper function of the digestive, immune, and endocrine systems; the brain and organs enjoy the regenerative results of increased blood-flow and oxygen; the bodymind finds its balance – finds its invitation for peace.

To come out of the pose, slowly bend the

knees, hugging them into the chest before rolling all the way over onto one side. Take a couple of deep breaths here, exhaling through the mouth, before gradually sitting upright again, seeing the world anew from a place of calm aliveness; from a place of healing.

Extended Asana Practice
Gomukhasana (Cow Face Pose)
Janu Sirsasana (Head to Knee Pose [Forward Bend and Revolved])
Bitilasana/Marjariasana (Cow Pose/Cat Pose)
Parsva Supta Vajrasana (Little Boat Twist)
Utthan Pristhasana (Lizard Pose)

Pranayama – Nadi Shodhana – Surya Nadi (Alternate Nostril Breathing – Solar Breath):

As Desikachar reminds us, the breath is the "intelligence of the body" – a means of whole-being awareness that, when engaged with, has the potential to both heal and transform. *Nadi Shodhana* is one such breathing technique designed to cleanse and purify the more than seventy-two-thousand *nadis* (energy channels) in the subtle body. In this version we will be

working with the *Pingala* or *Surya Nadi* – the
sun channel that spirals upwards from the base
of the spine into the right nostril. When we
practice the Solar Breath, inhaling and exhaling
exclusively through the sun channel, we warm
and energize the body, bringing action to
stagnation so that we can let go of our "inner
war" and find the confidence to choose and
affirm change in our lives.

Rest in a comfortable seated position, shrug
the shoulders back and down, and feel the spine
lengthen upwards as you root through the sits
bones, the belly loose and free. Using the *Vishnu
Mudra* (the hand gesture named after the
peace-loving Lord *Vishnu* – "The Sustainer" and
protector of life), in which the right index and
middle finger bend down so that their pads are
resting at the base of the palm, we use the right
pinkie and ring finger together to gently close
off the left nostril. Inhaling and exhaling fully
through the right nostril, the left remaining
closed off, continue for several rounds,
observing the energizing, clarifying feedback

from the bodymind as blockages release and balance is restored with the Solar Breath.

When you are ready, let the *Vishnu Mudra* fall away as the breath comes back to neutral. Sit for several moments in silence, watching. Feel radiant, renewed, receptive.

Dhyana – Abhyanga (Ayurvedic Self-Massage):

Abhyanga can become the shaping of a destiny, for, like a potter at the wheel, the power to transform literally lies in one's hands. The benefits of self-massage are profound: it increases circulation, stamina, muscle tone, joint lubrication, organ function, and detoxification, improves cell regeneration, vision, and sleep quality, calms the nervous system, and stabilizes over-stimulating emotional and mental energy. Taking up *abhyanga* is thus an expression of commitment to active healing – one of the highest forms of non-harm we can give to ourselves and others, as it is grounded in the recognition that our interconnectivity makes us as much accountable to the lives around us as we are to our own. Self-massage is therefore a form of meditation in and of itself.

In this version of *abhyanga*, instead of performing a traditional oil massage before we bathe, we use a bar of good-quality olive, sesame, coconut, or almond oil soap to massage the *marma* points (or areas of concentrated *prana* and vitality) in the body as we take our warm daily shower or bath. Beginning with the scalp, move your dry fingertips in a circular motion from the crown all the way around the head to the base of the skull. Lathering up the hands, move next to the face, gently massaging the chin, cheeks, and forehead before using the pads of the fingers to stroke away from the midline to the temples. Move on to the ears and lobes, finishing with the neck in an upward movement.

Re-lathering when necessary, continue on using firm caresses down the arms, pausing with a circular massage for the shoulders, elbows, and wrists. Spend extra time with each hand and areas of tenderness or tension. Using clockwise strokes across the chest and abdomen, finish the upper body with downward moving circular movements, using the thumbs to access tissue along the sides and middle to lower back. With the same pressure and downward strokes you used on the arms, caress the legs, taking time to massage out the seat muscles, hips, knees, ankles, and feet with circular motions.

As you perform the meditative ritual of *abhyanga* throughout your week or month, observe how such a simple act of self-care can become a measure of the quality of your life – of not only your experience of the world, but of how you are moved to respond to it. As you divine a new dimension of self from which to live an inner life from, feel how *you* become the gentle path itself.

Setting Intentions: Affirming the Capacity for Healing

I am the source and the course.

My thoughts, words, actions, habits, and character
are the caretakers of my destiny.

I make every choice as if an expressions of
gratitude, wonder, reverence, love, and healing.

I let go of pain and suffering
as an invitation for peace, healing, and transformation;
as a gesture of non-harm towards my self and all of life.

I accept the offering of a gentle path with
complete conviction that non-harm
is all the armor I will ever need.

~

~ Moving Inwards:
Meditations on Consciousness ~
Sutras 3.34-4.34:

3.34   *Samyama on the heart – the seat of wisdom – uncovers knowledge of the qualities of the mind.*

3.54   *Through samyama comes clarity – the ability to discern all within one's field of "that which is" with an encompassing understanding that is whole and free of obstructions. This is higher knowledge – a transcendent state of consciousness that is not acquired, but innate and intuitive to us all.*

3.55   *Through higher knowledge the mind becomes free, featureless; rather than the mind being master of the perceiver, the perceiver becomes master of the mind.*

4.25   *This clarity releases one from false identity; rather than asking who, what, where, why, and how am I, one simply understands "I am."*

4.31   *Through right-perception one becomes expansive, for there is nothing left to be known. This is Universal Consciousness – one's true nature, one's true Self.*

4.34   *Self-realization removes the divisions and distinctions of the mind, for there is no differentiation between "I" and "other"; all is One. Now end the teachings on the path to Yoga.*
     (Translation inspired by those of T. K. V. Desikachar and Swami Jnaneshvara Bharati)

~

Patanjali's *yamas* and *niyamas* serve as a compass for living an authentic life, and once we have set our course, there is no turning back. We have been forever changed, even by the briefest of glimpses at our promised horizon and the one certain truth that has been made available to us: that, to quote Desikachar, "We cannot see the color of the water in a lake if the lake is turbulent." In other words, to be whole is to be our Highest Self; to be a reflection rather than a fragmentation. The true nature of a body of water is stillness; unaffected, calm, it takes on the colour of the sky so much so that it can be difficult to tell one from the other. Likewise, in our own true nature of stillness, we experience the reality that *there is no differentiation between "I" and "other"; all is One. Universal Consciousness* rushes in; *one simply understands "I am"* – there is nothing more. We are the lake, and the sky.

This expansiveness, Patanjali argues, *is not acquired, but innate and intuitive* – available to us all, at all times. Arriving at it is a coming home to the Self, a remembering; we reencounter what it is to be free from associations, to be new again – like a child – as we commune through attentiveness and wonder with the Mystery that keeps presenting and representing itself to us. We become intimate once more with what it is to be present, with That which we feel unquestioningly a part of. This is *samyama*, the deep introspection of mindfulness (*dharaha*), meditation (*dhyana*), and oneness (*samadhi*) that returns us to the Essence we have always been. After our conscious movement (*asana*), breath work (*pranayama*), and ability to direct our attention inwards (*pratyahara*) begin to take on the shape of our destiny – of our course, our choice, and our character – we are called upon by *samyama* to continue along the lifelong journey towards Union.

Of the many objects and concepts Patanjali encourages us to focus this deep introspection on, the one that perhaps resonates most with Yoga as a process is Sutra 3.34, in which we are advised to align with the heart in order to truly know the mind. Such an illumination can seem entirely counterintuitive to a society convinced of the opposite: that intellect is prescribed by thought, not feeling. *Samyama on the heart* is not the confessional culture that has become its placeholder, nor is it the convenience of analysis and deconstruction; rather, deep introspection asks of us to do much more than the ego, shapeshifting as the heart, could ever do for us: it asks us to get out of the way; it asks us to stop asking questions.

"Be patient toward all that is unresolved in your heart and try to love the questions themselves," Rainer Maria Rilke once appealed. "Do not now seek the answers, which cannot be given you because you would not be able to live them. And the point is, to live everything." To know the mind, then, we must trust *the seat of wisdom*: the higher knowledge of the heart. This intelligence is not revealed through confession or analysis or deconstruction, but through being at peace with having questions and allowing their answers to present themselves to us by not asking them at all.

The understanding that we will only ever be given that which we are ready for and receptive to is complete liberation, for it becomes futile to do anything other that just be. Suddenly, the Buddhist proverb "when the student is ready, the teacher will appear" offers us a means of understanding the timing and meaning of that which we have faced in our lives. With expectation and judgment no longer relevant, the frenetic compulsion to worry or search or react falls away. As if returning to the sphere of the child, *whole and free from obstructions*, we begin to live life as if each encounter was the first of its kind. A mentality of potentiality allows us to *discern* rather than associate, to respond rather than react to the present moment. As Patanjali writes, *this clarity releases one from false identity* – from the *who, what, where, why, and how am I*. The great lesson of our lives, then, lies in the discovering and embracing anew of "*that which is*" and of all which "'*that*'" holds for us. Through deep introspection – the mindfulness, meditation, and Oneness of *samyama* that comprise Yoga's final three limbs – one comes to the humble realization "*I am*".

Samyama, then, is the re-education of the mind. Writer Mark Magill calls this process "taming the wild horse" – an analogy echoed in Patanjali's description of the *featureless* mind: without an agenda, it no longer serves itself, and *the perceiver becomes master*. Replacing the defaults and dulling rigidity of the mind is a sense of space and suppleness, giving to each moment the experience of a pure, ecstatic place. Oftentimes, this is one's first encounter with the Truth: that a *transcendent state of consciousness* is our essence, our bliss. Like an empty vessel we begin to receive everything as an offering, and it is within this recognition that doubt and resistance give way to gratitude, to celebration; we know we are where we are supposed to be, that we have the answers we are supposed to have. Hafiz once put it this way: "The place where you are right now/God circled on a map for you./Wherever your eyes and arms and heart can move/Against the earth and the sky,/ The Beloved has bowed there –/Our Beloved has bowed there knowing You were coming." Ultimately, to trust the lessons – the place where it was known we would arrive – means to trust their Source, and to trust the Source is to trust the *perceiver; there is no differentiation between "I" and "other"*, for in aligning with *Universal Consciousness* one recognizes that *all is One*. As Patanjali assures us, this *Self-realization removes the divisions and distinctions of the mind* that are a symptom of living externally, of projecting our lives outside of ourselves and thereby separating us from what is actually reflected in reality: the connection between all things – *Universal Consciousness*. Thus, with *right-perception one becomes expansive – one's true nature – for there is nothing left to be known*; we are within all things, and all things are within us, including the questions and the answers themselves. Zen Master Thich Nhat Hanh puts it this way: "We don't have to go anywhere/to obtain the truth./ We only need to be still/and things will reveal themselves/in the clear water of our heart."

Trust, then, is a channel, and it is through grounding in this Source that we are carried ashore from even the darkest of nights. This is the higher knowledge of the heart – a vocabulary of the soul buoyed by the joy of love. Living as an expression of this Truth, how we respond to each moment becomes an opportunity to be accountable to the needs of all beings – to the many facets of our Highest Self. To remember this connection in every thought, action, and word is to hear, see, and feel the Divine – to be an extension of the world's unfolding. This is what it means to be that which we have given – the meaning of life, as Vanda Scaravelli once avowed – and though we all may come to Yoga for different reasons, it is towards this end that the Yogic Path leads us.

Grounding Reflections: Developing Consciousness

~ In what ways do I need to realign with my heart, to reconnect with the insight, intuition, and intellect of feeling?

~ In what ways do I analyse and deconstruct "all that is unresolved" in my heart? What questions do I believe will be answered in doing this? Am I willing to stop asking these questions in order to "love" them instead?

~ In what ways am I willing to be "the student",
to trust that the lesson, the answer – "the
teacher" – will present itself to me when I am
ready and not when I think I am ready?

~ In what ways am I willing to accept that there
has been a timing and meaning behind all that I
have faced in my life? Am I willing to trust that I
am where I am supposed to be, and that I have
the answers I am supposed to have – even if I
am living through "the darkest of nights"?

~ In what ways am I ready to ground in the
Source, to embrace the needs of all beings as
the needs of my self knowing that all is an
extension of the world's unfolding – an
expression of the Divine?

Supporting Practices: Deepening Consciousness

Asana, Pranayama, & Dhyana – Yoga Nidra
(Yogic Sleep):

   The *Yoga Nidra* is an invitation into alert rest.
As we integrate the bodymind and breath
through conscious awareness, we move towards
our centre and a deepening sense of relaxation
that lifts away division.

   Consciousness comes to rest within the

sensing body. Lying back comfortably, with legs straight and arms at your side, close the eyes and allow the heavy body to surrender towards the support of the earth beneath you. Feel the cool tide of the breath as it enters, following its warmth as it leaves, the whole body slowly rising and falling like a wave as you continue. Notice the peaceful drum of the heart, the shades and shadows passing over the eyelids, the tastes, scents, sounds, sensations, or lack of sensations that are present with you now. Become attentive to any areas of holding or tension, and give them permission to let go. The jaw rests back, the lips are soft, the brow is smooth. With each exhale the shoulder blades widen away from each other, finding space, while the low-back lengthens downwards as it slowly kisses the ground.

Consciousness comes to rest within the right foot and leg. On an in-breath, tense and squeeze all of the muscles in the leg, pointing the toes, and on an out-breath, letting them go, feeling their weight release back into the floor, relaxed and at ease.

Consciousness comes to rest within the left foot and leg. On an in-breath, tense and squeeze all of the muscles in the leg, pointing the toes, and on an out-breath, letting them go, feeling their weight release back into the floor, relaxed and at ease.

Consciousness comes to rest within the back of the body. On an inhale, tense and squeeze all of the seat muscles surrounding the pelvis, holding, and on an exhale, letting them go, feeling their weight release into the floor as the lumbar sinks down, relaxed and at ease.

Consciousness comes to rest within the front of the body. On an inhale, allow the belly and chest to expand, filling out, and on an exhale, letting them go, feeling their weight release into the thoracic as it grounds, relaxed and at ease.

Consciousness comes to rest within the right arm and hand. Inhaling, tense and squeeze all of the muscles in the arm, clenching the fingers into the palm, and exhaling, letting them go, feeling their weight release back into the floor, relaxed and at ease.

Consciousness comes to rest within the left arm and hand. Inhaling, tense and squeeze all of the muscles in the arm, clenching the fingers into the palm, and exhaling, letting them go, feeling their weight release back into the floor, relaxed and at ease.

Consciousness comes to rest within the face and throat. Inhaling, tense and squeeze all of the muscles in the face, tucking the chin in gently as the crown lengthens up through the cervical, and exhaling, letting them go, feeling the weight of the head as it grounds and the face and throat soften, relaxed and at ease.

Consciousness comes to rest within the expressive body. Observe, without attachment, any emotions that present themselves or fall away, any thoughts, images, or sounds colouring your internal landscape, before letting them go as the mind and mood settle, relaxed and at ease.

Consciousness comes to rest within the energetic body. Observe, without attachment, any pranic shifts that present themselves or fall away as you bring your attention down through the chakras, beginning with crown centre (the top of the head), moving to third eye centre (between the brows), throat centre (between the collar bone and chin), heart centre (at the middle of the sternum), navel centre (above the belly button), hara centre (bellow the belly button), and root centre (at the base of the spine). Letting go of the chakras on an exhale, feel the body open and receptive, while relaxed and at ease.

Consciousness comes to rest within the essential body. Observe, without attachment, the still, silent space at your centre as you come home to your Self – to your essence. Allow your entire being to become an expression of this Divine light and the joyful expansiveness of bliss, peace, purity, loving-kindness, and knowingness that is your true nature. Inhaling from the base of the spine up to the crown of the head, and exhaling from the crown back down through the spine to its base, continue to ground in this inner source as it sweeps through and sustains you. Letting go of the spinal breath, feel the many layers of self relaxed and at ease.

Consciousness comes to rest, once again, within the sensing body. Returning to the everyday, slowly reawaken movement by taking time to gently stretch the fingers, toes, arms, and legs before coming up into a comfortable seated position. Feeling nourished and whole, open the eyes when you are ready, knowing that this deep-seated sense of transcendental balance and wellbeing is always available as you carry it with you throughout the rest of your day.

Extended Asana Practice
Ardha Pincha Mayurasana (Dolphin Pose)
Prasarita Padottanasana (Wide Legged Standing Forward Bend Sequence)
Ardha Chandrasana (Half Moon Pose)
Anjaneyasana (Crescent Moon Pose [High or Low Lunge])
Hasta Padangusthasana (Upright Big Toe Sequence)

Setting Intentions: Affirming Consciousness

My true nature is a reflection, a remembering;
I am the lake, and the sky.

When I align with the heart, I get out of the way of the
questions in order to hear its answers.

I am *featureless*, an empty vessel;
freed from conditioning,
I receive everything as an offering
knowing that I can only hold what I need.

I live a vocabulary of the soul; I respond to the world
– to all expressions of the Divine –
with joy, wonder, gratitude, and love.

My trust is a channel;
I ground in *Universal Consciousness*.

I live knowing that I am all that I have given.

When I am Whole, I *am*.

~

Sources & Works Cited

Amon, Nissim. *Healing Rhythms: 15 Steps to Relax, Relieve, and Restore.* With Andrew Weil and Dean Ornish. Mentors Channel: Mobilize Your Wellbeing. Web. 6 May 2015. http://www.mentorschannel.com/WildDivine/HealingRhythms/LandingPage/

Angelou, Maya. The Things We Say. Web. 6 May 2015. http://www.thethingswesay.com/do-the-best-you-can-until-you-know-better-then-when-you-know-better-do-better/

Ban Breathnach, Sarah. *Simple Abundance: A Daybook of Comfort and Joy.* New York, New York, USA: Warner Books, 1995.

Basho, Matsuo. Trans. Robert Bly. *The Poetry Dictionary.* 2nd ed. By John Drury. Ed. Michelle Ruberg Ehrhard. Cincinnati, Ohio, USA: Writer's Digest Books, 2006.

Bertherat, Thérèse. *The Body Has Its Reasons: Self-Awareness Through Conscious Movement.* With Carol Bernstein. Rochester, Vermont, USA: Healing Arts Press, 1989.

Bharati, Jnaneshvara. "Yoga Sutras of Patanjali - Raja Yoga - Ashtanga Yoga." *Yoga Sutras.* Traditional Yoga and Meditation of the Himalayan Masters: Self-Realization through the Yoga Sutras, Vedanta, Samaya Sri Vidya Tantra. Web. 6 May 2015. http://www.swamij.com/yoga-sutras.htm

Brown, Christina. *The Yoga Bible: A Definitive Guide to Yoga Postures*. Cincinnati, Ohio, USA: Walking Stick Press, 2003.

Bryne, Robert. "Robert Bryne." goodreads. Web. 6 May 2015. http://www.goodreads.com/author/show/1707476.Robert_Bryne

Chopra, Deepak. *The Book of Secrets: Unlocking the Hidden Dimensions of Your Life*. New York, New York, USA: Three Rivers Press, 2004.

Coulter, H. David. *Anatomy of Hatha Yoga: A Manual for Students, Teachers, and Practitioners*. Honesdale, Pennsylvania, USA: Body and Breath, 2001.

Das, Surya. *Awakening the Buddha Within: Eight Steps to Enlightenment: Tibetan Wisdom for the Western World*. New York, New York, USA: Broadway Books, 1997.

Desikachar, T. K. V. *The Heart of Yoga: Developing a Personal Practice*. Rochester, Vermont: Inner Traditions International, 1995.

Desmond, Andy (Miten). *The Spirit of Mantra with Deva Premal and Miten: 21-Day Mantra Meditation Journey Vol. II*. Mentors Channel: Mobilize Your Wellbeing. Web. 6 May 2015. http://www.mentorschannel.com/DevaPremal/21-DayMantraMeditationJourneyII/Online/

Elgin, Duane. *Voluntary Simplicity: Toward a Way of Life That Is Outwardly Simple, Inwardly Rich*. New York, New York, USA: Quill, 1993.

Farhi, Donna. *Teaching Yoga: Exploring the Teacher-Student Relationship*. Berkeley, California, USA: Rodmell Press, 2006.

Frawley, David. *Yoga and Ayurveda: Self-Healing and Self-Realization*. Twin Lakes, Wisconsin, USA: Lotus Press, 1999.

Gilbert, Elizabeth. *Eat, Pray, Love: One Woman's Search for Everything Across Italy, India, and Indonesia*. London, England, UK: Penguin Books, 2006.

Hafiz. Trans. Daniel Ladinsky. *The Gift: Poems by Hafiz, the Great Sufi Master*. New York, New York, USA: Penguin Compass, 1999.

---. Trans. Daneil Ladinsky. *The Subject Tonight is Love: 60 Wild and Sweet Poems of Hafiz*. New York, New York, USA: Penguin Compass, 1996.

Hay, Louise L. *Heal Your Body A-Z: The Mental Causes for Physical Illness and the Metaphysical Way to Overcome Them*. Carlsbad, California, USA: Hay House, 1988.

Isaacs, Nora. "The Upside of Ego." *Yoga Journal*. March 2014.

Lad, Vasant. *The Complete Book of Ayurvedic Home Remedies*. New York, New York, USA: Three Rivers Press, 1998.

MacLean, Marina. *Ayurvedic Meditations*. Peterborough, Ontario, Canada: self-published, 2014.

---. *Marina MacLean Yoga Registered Yoga School: 200 Hours Yoga Teacher Training*. Peterborough, Ontario, Canada: self-published, 2012.

---. *Soma: Nectar of Rejuvenation*. Peterborough, Ontario, Canada: self-published, 2014.

Magill, Mark. *Why is the Buddha Smiling?: Mindfulness as a Means of Bringing Calm and Insight to Your Life*. Gloucester, Massachusetts, USA: Fair Winds Press, 2003.

Malebranche, Nicolas. *Illuminations: Essays and Reflections*. By Walter Benjamin. Trans. Harry Zohn. Ed. Hannah Arendt. New York, New York, USA: Harcourt, Brace & World, 1968.

Morningstar, Amadea and Urmila Desai. *The Ayurvedic Cookbook: A Personalized Guide to Good Nutrition and Health*. Twin Lakes, Wisconsin, USA: Lotus Press, 1990.

Myers, Esther. *Yoga and You: Energizing and Relaxing Yoga for New and Experienced Students*. Toronto, Ontario, Canada: Random House of Canada, 1996.

Myss, Caroline. *Anatomy of the Spirit: The Seven Stages of Power and Healing*. New York, New York, USA: Harmony Books, 1996.

Nhat Hanh, Thich. *Moments of Mindfulness: Daily Inspiration*. Berkeley, California, USA: Parallax Press, 2013.

Osho. *Meditation for Busy People*. Mentors Channel: Mobilize Your Wellbeing. Web. 6 May 2015. http://www.mentorschannel.com/Osho/ MeditationforBusyPeople/

Ray, Veronica. *Green Spirituality: Reflections on Belonging to a World Beyond Myself*. Center City, Minnesota, USA: Hazelden, 1992.

Rilke, Rainer Maria. *Letters to a Young Poet*. New York, New York, USA: W. W. Norton, 1934.

Scaravelli, Vanda. *Awakening the Spine: The Stress-Free New Yoga that Works with the Body to Restore Health, Vitality and Energy*. New York, New York: HarperOne, 1991.

Tolle, Eckhart. *A New Earth: Awakening to Your Life's Purpose*. New York, New York, USA: Plume, 2006.

Vanzant, Iyanla. *One Day My Soul Just Opened Up: 40 Days and 40 Nights Toward Spiritual Strength and Personal Growth*. New York, New York, USA: Fireside, 1998.

*"I would love to live
Like a river flows,
Carried by the surprise
Of its own unfolding."*
~ John O'Donohue

Erin Holtz Braeckman's yoga journey has been an unfolding –
one that has carried her over nearly fifteen years, beginning
first as a student seeking to rediscover lightness and freedom
in her body. Yoga has since been a constant and a passion in
her life, leading her to complete in 2012 her RYT 200
certification in Hatha Yoga with longstanding teacher and
mentor Marina MacLean, E-RYT 500. She is now a registered
instructor with Yoga Alliance and teaches out of her home
studio, The Village Yoga Studio, in Lakefield, Ontario.

Erin also holds a Bachelor of Arts (Trent University) and a
Master of Arts (Trent University) in English Literature, as well
as a Bachelor of Education (Queen's University). She is a part-
time Special Education Teacher and is a member of the
faculty at Lakefield College School, where she coinstructs the
Yoga Program and incorporats the breathing, meditation, and
stretching practices of Hatha Yoga into her classroom.

When not in the studio, reading an inspiring book, travelling,
cooking, volunteering, grounding in and promoting spiritual
wellness, or writing with pen in hand, Erin can be found
outside communing with her garden or enjoying the
nourishing company of her young son, her husband, her
friends, family, pets - and other beings.

Namaste.

ॐ

CPSIA information can be obtained at www.ICGtesting.com
Printed in the USA
LVOW10s1145040716

495050LV00007B/18/P